C000226359

STREET BALLADS

George Barker was born in Essex in 1913. His first
book of poems was published by Faber and Faber in
1935, and his *Collected Poems*, including work from
the numerous volumes he produced since then,
appeared under the same imprint in 1987. *Street
Ballads*, his first subsequent volume, is published
posthumously. After many years of foreign domicile, in
Japan, America and Italy, George Barker returned to
England, and lived in Norfolk until his death in
October 1991.

by the same author

POEMS OF PLACES AND PEOPLE (1971)
IN MEMORY OF DAVID ARCHER (1973)
DIALOGUES, ETC. (1976)
VILLA STELLAR (1978)
ANNO DOMINI (1983)
COLLECTED POEMS (1987)

STREET BALLADS

George Barker

faber and faber
LONDON · BOSTON

First published in 1992
by Faber and Faber Limited
3 Queen Square London WC1N 3AU

Photoset by Wilmaset Ltd, Birkenhead, Wirral
Printed in Great Britain by
Cox and Wyman Ltd, Reading, Berkshire

All rights reserved

© George Barker, 1992

George Barker is hereby identified as author of
this work in accordance with Section 77 of the
Copyright, Designs and Patents Act 1988

*This book is sold subject to the condition that it shall not,
by way of trade or otherwise, be lent, resold, hired out or
otherwise circulated without the publisher's prior consent in
any form of binding or cover other than that in which it is
published and without a similar condition including this
condition being imposed on the subsequent purchaser*

A CIP record for this book is available from the British Library

ISBN 0-571-16609-1

2 4 6 8 10 9 7 5 3 1

To James Edward Francis

It is not a question of a search for disinterested intellectual truth, but of a personal choice involving guilt and dread rather than blindness and ignorance.

R. Grindley, *On Kierkegaard's Fear & Trembling*

Contents

Acknowledgements

I would wish to express my acknowledgements to Mr Michael Schmidt of the Carcanet Press, Mr Anthony Astbury of the Greville Press, Alicia Hull, Mr Hedley Marten, and to Raffaella and Hugh St Clair. And my gratitude to the Royal Literary Fund for its generosity.

Ben Bulben Revisited

Lie still, old man, lie still,
Nothing's here to disturb you.
The ghosts are gone, the heroes
Lie snoring under the hill.
And the sea-bedded hoydens
That used so to perturb you,
Yes, you and your monkey gland,
Now sleep and never feel
The hallowing in your hand.
But now the beast is real
Slouching from Nazareth
With death under its elbow
And filthy on its breath
The ordure of Armageddon.

Old man, old man of the mountain
Only us silly sheep
Wander over the mountain
To populate your sleep.
The statesmen they may rave
And the soldiers roar
And old Adam behave
As foolishly as before –
Now that we take our leave
Of every thing we have,
There is nothing to save
Old man, any more,
Only, only the ground and the grave
And the angel at the door.

Old man, old dreaming man
Dream us also asleep
And then perhaps we can
Somehow manage to keep
The dream with which we began:
That vision of walking through
The common or garden wood
Until we came home to
The knowledge of evil and good
Wherein, like a holy house
We sat down at last
And found ourselves free to choose
An agape, or feast
With the black mystical beast.

Was it no more than a dream
This holy house of knowledge
In which we seemed to seem
At liberty to encourage
Either evil or good? Time
And the triumphant fiend
Have blown the house down
Bombed and blasted and blown
The homely house down
And now nothing remains
For all our many pains
Save us and a few ruins,
Neither evil nor good,
Only wrack and the wreckage,
And where old Adam stood
Only the brute and its carnage.
Sleep on, old man, among

The ruins and the echoes,
The small lies and the great rimes,
The stones and the rocky poems,
For they at least belong
By the Ben Bulben of dreams.

Vale Kavanagh

I

.I remember a foulmouthed Irish labourer
    with a head like a prophet's
and a tongue as racy and as dirty as
    his personal habits.

II

He was as dishonest as only an honest
    man can be
who finds himself dying between the devil and
    the Irish Sea.

III

What odd event has transformed this piece of
    Inishkeen sod
into an effigy remarking: 'I think
    I'm becoming a god'?

IV

Birds of a feather we were, my dear Paddy,
    my own nest just as foul
as yours or indeed as any man's
    with half a soul.

V

Let them wash you white as they will, Kavanagh,
    we come from dirt and from dust
and the dust and the dirt animates us all
    as thank god it must.

VI

Fortunately poets, like poems, are often dirty
   and brutish and short
but somehow I think that the gods, perhaps,
   may spare us a thought.

For Patrick Swift

Patrick Swift, for whom I write
these long delayed lines in a night
given over to bad dreams and broken
images, I tender these words as token
to your green memory, if speech
like a homing pigeon can reach
you in the lightning-shrouded, stark
and final backyard of the dark.
I think it may, for there's a sense
in which the lost intelligence
illuminates and visits spheres
it neither knows, believes or hears
but like the bird tied at a stake
feels a flight it cannot make.
And so into six feet of ground
I have descended, and have found
and silently addressed the bone
that in turn speaks to my own.
Can you, Swift, like a flint spark
strike up from the gravelled dark
illuminating the obscurity
of vacuous eternity?
(The whistling whispering Swift would
if any could, if any could.)
I saw and heard his word walk over
water and wilderness, and uncover
mysteries that had long lain hid
under the spiritual pyramid.
I heard him charm the sacred snake

down from its branch, and saw him take
ideals by the hand and show
them how to peacock to and fro.
'The theology of the object, this
animates everything that is.'
The brush that he held in his hand
sign and symbol, instrument and
artillery of his graphic will
never, for me, performed as well
as that bright goldfishing diver
his tongue: it fished from the river
secrets only nature seemed
to know or the swift mind dreamed.
The dawn comes up as I write this
and in its own way this verse is
to thank Ireland for her gift
to us of the painter Patrick Swift:
for Kavanagh's honesty, Yeats
for the great images he creates
for Synge, for MacNeice, for Joyce
for Sam Beckett and all warty boys.
Yes, let some decent praise be sung
and for Swift, the Golden Tongue.

The Borstal Boy

This boy has broken out of that
odd public school by name Borstal.
The police are after him and when
they get him he'll know what's what.

The Borstal Boy is on the run.
He really thinks that he can hide
in a ditch by an open field.
He does not know what he has done.

He has red hair and thinks he can
talk sensibly to cows and horses.
Why? He trusts them. He trusts tractors. He
does not trust his fellow man.

The police claim he stole a car.
He has a way with old machines.
He does not know the arm of the law
can reach very fast and far.

He sleeps almost every night in a
corrugated-covered ditch.
He keeps a twenty-two air rifle.
He shoots pheasants for his dinner.

The parson does his simple best
to talk him into going back
to Borstal but the boy can not
perceive the need for his arrest.

I saw him yesterday beside
the river, stalking with his gun
a pheasant gaudy as a prince.
I heard it shriek out as it died.

Sonnet: For a Friend

Drink. Drugs. Women. Death.
Four best of things to be desired:
Four little foibles that we shared,
The four archangels of our faith.
'Let us,' we said, 'just for a joke
experiment with experience.'
And when the abused spirit broke
under the savaging of sense
we heard the voices of those four
evangelists start whistling like
fried lark tongues shrieking on a fire
and the drink and the drugs and the women and death
sang up like sirens from the rocks.
Who is it that their singing mocks?

The Procreations of Eve and
the Copulations of Adam

The child that from the tear of Eve's
    snake- and knowledge-haunted eyes
sprang down, now for ever grieves
    to return to paradise.

Out of the homicidal heart
    of Adam the fleshed horn
sprang up and tore his breast apart
    and god knows what was born.

Street Ballad

As I lay by the summer Tiber I heard the fishes singing:
'Down here they do not ring the bell of hell on Sunday
  morning,
nor do all the bones get up and walk like sheep to
  slaughter.
Down here we swim in lovely sin as sweet as holy water.
O what paradise on earth it is to play about in
the fountain of the Holy See, O see the holy fountain!

The Holy Church sees to it that all fishes in the Tiber
are kept well fed, put clean to bed and mustn't read the
  Bible.
And if you ask us why the Church is so concerned with
  fish
we must reply: 'Because we are the Church's favourite
  dish.'

Street Ballad

Somewhere in the past there is a vacant room
    and there, on a bed of thorn
lies the one I should have been, who was
    never even born.

Haunted by all those things I should have been
    had I been him,
why does his innocence tear at my heart like wild
    flesh-eating cherubim?

The Suicides

Ulrike Meinhof
Andreas Baader
Jan-Carle Raspe
Gudrun Ensslin
died in Stuttgart-
Stammheim prison
October nineteen
seventy seven.
The powers that be
have never decided
whether their deaths
were murders or
four suicides.
It seems a little
unlikely that
— just as statistics —
the four of them did it
at the same time
in separate cells.
And Bobby Sands
hunger striker
political prisoner
Irish patriot
pronounced by
Margaret Thatcher
'to have committed
suicide by starving
himself to death'. So
much for them

the suicides.
Forget them.
Shall we forget them?
Forget them. Forget them.
The suicides.

Rosie and Benny in a Taxicab 1983

And Benny looked at Rosie
    and he said:
'You are taking me to the Middlesex Hospital
    and in half an hour I shall be dead.'

And Rosie looked at Benny with
    a knowing eye,
'You are taking me to the Middlesex Hospital
    and in six weeks I shall die.'

It is a sad fact that what both Rosie and Benny
    said was true.
Very soon both had gone. I suppose
    both of them knew.

For in the cab poor Benny was axed
    with some kind of stroke.
He was carried into the hospital and
    never moved or spoke.

Rosie knocked around for a bit
    then took some stuff
that snuffed her out. She felt
    she'd had enough.

This is for my daughter Rosie and Young Benny
    and anyone else
who sometimes in taxicabs has overheard
    the jingle bells.

A Version of Animula Vagula Blandula

I know where you are now. But do you know?
Are you here in this word? I have not heard
you whistling in the dark. Do not allow
the noun or pronoun or the verb to disturb you.
Sometimes, I think that death is really no joke
but then I have died only two or three such times.
Perhaps there is always someone to attend the
absconding mountebank. But you, farewelling ghost,
    poor
imperial little thing, go you alone?
Go you alone to the altering? Or am I with you?

Street Ballad

Nothing was wasted. Not a word.
    Not a spittle of poison.
Not the knife in the back, not the salt in the wound,
    Not a wound of the passion.

Here in my heart may the monument
    Of every moment remain.
At Halicarnassus Mausolus
    Also remembers the pain.

On Wittgenstein's 'That Which Cannot Be Spoken Of' etc.

or 'I gotta use words when I talk to you'

I

Here it is again. Here it is again. Here it is,
all that which is not and will never be
ordered into the verbal synthesis
where A precedes X and I cannot write C.
And in a dream I saw the primal ape
mouthing the message that it could not utter:
The shamble of moithering would not take shape.
The wretched primate tried its best to mutter:
'To guess I ought not, really, even try.'
And Ludwig in his tomb began to speak
like a tongue-tied evangelist, explaining why
we cannot explain. Jesus Christ, it's Greek.

II

'Language is the discourse of the soul with herself.'
Plato, *Theaetetus*

A thought, perhaps as of a fading torch
flickers up in the corridors of the mind
and I see them, sprawled upon the floor,
spreadeagled on the wall, piled up like
dead fish that sliver and flash in the beam
of dying light, the denizens that expire in the head
without a word; they exude a putrescence
like the blue glare of gas, these rotting forms

that once flashed and flickered
in the streams of the imagination
and the memory. Now they lie here
the walking and shuddering words that dig or have dug
their own stench of a grave where they now die.
The purpose of this hideous necrosis?
The mind breeds its ideas as the heap
of dead leaves breeds ephemera and exuviae
but these alas only too seldom burst forth
to ignite the poem's fire.

Critical Sonnet for William Shakespeare

> Anon, as patient as the female dove,
> When that her golden couplets are disclos'd,
> His silence will sit drooping.
>
> > *Hamlet* v:i

What most I wish to hear from you I heard.
It was the silence in between the speaking,
the golden silences that charged the word
with correspondences I had been seeking
in all vocables. But only your
silences like the patient female dove
disclosed the secret I had been looking for:
language is the golden cage of our love.

It is as though the heart, adoring silence
but tortured by the ghouls of its existence,
cried out howling in the night, or sang
wildly of love in dreams of violence,
or till its suffering, cracked at the final pang,
out of the dead mouths of children rang.

On a Bird Dead in the Road

What formerly flounced and flew its fantastic feathers
Now lies like a flattened old leather glove in the road,
And the gigantic wheels of the articulated juggernaut
   lorries
Pound down on it all day long like the mad will of god.

Street Ballad

There, by the falling water
    in which we turn to stone
for ever the infant dances
beyond the imperfect tenses
    in which we turn to stone.

There in its clouds and roses
    that cannot ever die
with tongues of fire that infant
chants the everlasting instant
    that cannot die.

Ikons

To Edward

I

But was there time? No.
    There was never time.
There was only the breath
exhaled by the first burning
babe from a cloud, lasting
the whole of one flaming moment
before the ashes fell.

II

Where was the place? The place
    was not here.
Some far where else the
    celebration of bells,
      the house of sacred things,
the rider on the bull, the dying
    serpent's tears,
the peacock crying
and, like knives in the sky,
    extraordinary wings.

III

Can I come back to you?
    No one is there.
They are all gone. No one was
    ever there.

The mask of the holy man has
      faded now and
the silence is not golden.
      Through love shall we
labour to give birth to
      death, when the fiery
mountain and the inverted
      dog inherit the earth.

                    IV

Who was there? No one was
      ever there, where
the hands meet at midnight and
      the wave, breaking,
hangs for ever over
      rocks that cannot speak. There
you will find a face staring
      out of eyes
that cannot see the sea.

                    V

The leopard may sleep in chains
      and the nebula
bare a sunburst in its
      breast but
no dreams attend those cold
      lairs, no bone
grows from the grave there,
but sleeping, the gleam of the phoenix
      in the spread of its sunburst
dreams of old bones.

VI

And over October fields a single
    death stalks out of its life into
a river of subterranean springs.
    Haunted by knowledge it walks
into the lunar and erotic cave.
    And then the scarecrow speaks
of love to a ghost in the laurel grove.

VII

Whose blood drips from the engines? Whose?
    Overhead I hear the crack of
    February glass and the lightning
    dance in November coffins.
    Five loves
multiply zeros and crosses in the air
and where I seek you, find
wounds, only wounds with wings,
    wounds like knives.

VIII

Who are those apes sedulously
    re-setting type
that no one can ever read? Apples
    appear at the tips
of the god's fingers
    then deflate like bladders
because we know
    Laiki has always murdered
golden Apollo. These
    the images of eternal impermanence.

IX

Whose was the voice? From
       far-off effigies
I hear the lyrics of
       those Grecian liars who
died for information.
       Will the table rise flapping
like an open book in the air
       and the alphabet, in a dance,
in a trance, continually declare
       the word is love, but there
is no word there.

X

Later the moon, rising over Russia
drew pyramidical constructions
       of white skulls out of
the steppes of the past, until I thought
I gazed upon philosophical battlements
dividing Europe and the hordes of bones
battling behind my eyes. Then
among those fallen I came upon my star.

XI

The lesser mysteries always contain the greater
just as the zero multiplies or the circle
retreats into the recurring seven to leave us
wandering along a seacoast where Isaac Newton
       contemplating pebbles
takes by the arm a winged Victory that whispers:
       'Every one is everyone today.'

XII

I have not learned the ceremonies of salvation
if they are not like this. They go,
the young dog dancing after old Adam,
and the flayed babe singing,
and Aphrodite, her belly full of cupids,
alighting tiptoe upon rocks,
all ceaselessly chanting in flames, ceaselessly chanting.

To Catullus

Of all men tenderest, living, loving Veronan
receiving as I have from the hand of a friend
those verses which in truth are not so much poems
as the heavenly menagerie of the human heart
it is not, no, never on any bookshelf
I with a cold hand place your living urn
(how could one use such poems in that fashion?)
but bury it in the deserted sands of my spirit
where, blossoming every day it will bring sunrise.

To Yu-Tsan

Yu-Tsan, loveliest of jades
    or water lilies,
lilies of the field, lilies of the fern
    lily of the valleys

how can I ever believe
    that you, heart of my heart
lily of all lilies, cost as little as
    any other tart?

At the Waterfall of Tivoli

It is not the fake figures or the falsifying
facts or the unforgivable fabrications of
fools or even the rhetorical
rodomontade violently ravishing
the divine veritas in an invented
inversion; nor is it the vanishing visionary, raving
as carried off into clouds by an
exact exaggeration; nor is it
the christened and crucified Krishna
imitating a near myth, or the mynah bird calling up
a cloud-cuckoo India nor the word of
vacuous thunder belabouring heaven
for that forgotten password paradise
itself has passed over, or the motor-car salesman
or the parson who composes a prayer of self-pity
as he palavers in praise of perished pisgahs;
or those who speak of the tooth of Buddha
in candy; or those who describe
artificial trees in uninhabited landscapes
nor the simple soul faking for favour, not the
flashing scoundrel adorning his chapel with prizes
or the prosperous politician regurgitating specious shit
    nor
even those who protest they befriend
the endless enemy; nor the Lyre Bird;
not the pronged tongue or the Fabulae
frenzied falsehood fighting for life or death

knowing that it breeds both. No, none of these.
The lie can be spoken only by the waterfall
that issues from the fissures of the ravined Tivoli.
For it alone speaks, it alone knows the truth.

Jan 2nd 1989: Aubade

I

When the horses of old Plato
    stir towards the chariot
and the wise philosopher
    starts re-thinking what's what,
when the heart, from its sinning
    turns towards the whitewashed sky
of a bright new day beginning
    like a kaleidoscopic lie,
when the cock stands up as red
    as the horny head and ball
and the huntress in her bed
    turns towards the bridal wall
and from her exhausted hand
    lets the head of Eros fall,
when the feline soul creeps in
    from her night in the guttered stews
dreaming of a love as steamy
    as the New York Daily News:
then the ordinary day
    for all ordinary people
rings out like an ordinary
    bell from a steeple.

II

At the Walpurgisnacht of the soul
that miserable delusion sits
beside itself muttering: 'I suffer –
but do I exist?'

O laurel tree: O laurel tree!
The invincible machines, the
ironic engines, the great generators:
Will the landscape explode if I
cease to believe in it?

Into the mind that sits alone
to contemplate its emptiness
as I by rivers have looked down
at waters where a face should be
and seen nothing but black sky,
so into the glass bowl between
the silence of the ears I see
invisible islands congregate,
huge headless cephaloids multiply
and absence walk upon the void
like deathwatch beetles. It is the
mind staring into its last breath
upon the cracked glass as it sees
all things that it believed in pass
into vacuity.

The Eight Voyages of Sanctimonious Bones

The First Voyage of Sanctimonious Bones

'O voluble ghost of Sanctimonious Bones
    whither O whither away?'
'What do you care where I go?
    What do you care what I say?'

The palm tree flirts, the boys wear skirts.
    The sharks smoke cigars by the shore.
By the glare of the moon in the lazy lagoon
    the whale fountains up with each snore.

'By old Davy Jones!' Sanctimonious Bones
    cried: 'I care not a fig for my life
If I can achieve, by next Christmas Eve
    sanctimoniousness or a wife.'

Through tropical zones Sanctimonious Bones
    sailed away in pursuit of his fate.
He dared Polar Seas, Heligolands, Hebrides
    in search of a mass or a mate.

(But the man is liable to be undesirable.
    He teaches worse things than he preaches
And these are to tarry rather than marry
    and to lounge around on the beaches.)

For Sanctimonious Bones is felonious.
    He is doomed like the Flying Dutchmen
To wander abroad, for no wife or reward
    will ever decorate such men.

The Second Voyage of Sanctimonious Bones

As Captain Bones bestrode the deck
    he felt the timbers shiver:
'But why does she quake? Why does she shake?
    I'm sailing up a river.'

So sweet and smooth the path to truth
    if you sail up the Tiber
(unlike the Sutra or the Brahmaputra
    or rowing over the Khyber).

All rivers come home at last to Rome
    and all known roads as well:
For she does not quibble, the Roman Sibyl,
    she simply contradicts Hell.

'Ah,' quoth the Angel, 'This is so,
    but if you sail in reverse
The path's the same but you'll end in the flame
    of Hellfire, only worse.'

The Third Voyage of Sanctimonious Bones

As I walked down Kensington High Street
    one rainy Friday evening
I realized that I had devised
    no method for love or believing.

The spectre of youth spoke no word of truth,
    the laws of love in suspense
Hung like old rags or Department Store flags
    and nothing made any sense.

Then not too loud but out of a cloud
    a voice like a bookmaker's shouted:
'I have a cure for the cad, the impure
    and all silly sods who have doubted.'

And from my heart, like a ragged upstart
    rose the whisper: 'O tell me what
I must do to respond to this dark despond-
    ency, for I know not.'

'O take your soul, like a goldfish bowl
    and place it upon your head,
Then think not of loss but intrepidly cross
    the dangerous road,' it said.

'And do not spill one drop until
    you reach the other side.
Dare the dregs and the drabs, the buses, the cabs
    and also the rain,' it cried.

So I balanced the whole glass goldfish bowl
        like a globe upon my head
And without spilling a drop, or a fish, did not stop
        that treacherous track to tread.

And now I sit as happy as it
        is possible to be
With the goldfish bowl of my old fish soul
        safe for eternity.

The Fourth Voyage of Sanctimonious Bones

To what was I turning when I was burning?
        Well, I was yearning for Carthage.
On my back Sin, on my gob a grin,
        and no soul at all for portage.

I looked all around at that sacrosanct ground
        hoping to find Saint Augustine
Sitting as neat as a ghost in a sheet
        and ready to answer the question.

But only the vast Sahara at last
        with a distant echo responded:
'We are very sorry – it's rather a worry –
        Augustine has absconded.'

Is it deserted? Is it unconverted
    the region he now inhabits
With nobody there but God and a pair
    of extremely infertile rabbits?

Alone, alone, like Livingstone
    with a halo where his face is,
For where he sits's not a desert it's
    an entirely holy oasis.

O if I could swim I would join him
    where he sits collating agenda
And if I'd been taught to walk on the water
    I'd sit there with him in his splendour.

The Fifth Voyage of Sanctimonious Bones

As I sailed around in circles
    on the Everlasting Bay
I saw all gods, all, all the old sods
    as happy as the day.

They sang and danced, they danced and sang
    a doxological song:
'From East to West we are the best
    happy as day is long.'

But thunder banged about the world
    the ocean rose and roared
The wind went wild, the ship capsized,
    and I fell overboard.

Did the Divinities relapse
    into a state of shock
And cast me just a bit of string
    or Peter from a rock?

They danced and sang, they sang and danced
    like angels all around.
I sank three times in the holy sea.
    and there and then I drowned.

O had they cast a rope of hope
    or even that bit of string
I would be at work in the little kirk.
    They did not do a thing.

They danced and sang, they sang and danced
    so, underneath the wave
I leave them all to their festival
    and they me to my grave.

The Sixth Voyage of Sanctimonious Bones

I am the spectre of Bones. The rector
    of Walsingham Church baptized me.
For what it's worth, well, at my birth
    the holy ghost chastised me.

I then took to sea, to fly, to flee
    from that apparition appalling:
I was in the lurch. Cash, not church
    was all I ever heard calling.

So many choirs attended the fires
    of heaven and of hell
That I did not know which way to go:
    fared ill my farewell.

I chased the ghost from pillar to post
    of Rome and theologies vaster.
I'm an active man, but fast as I ran
    the gods ran away even faster.

We are now at sea. Since you and me
    are only here on probation
Shall we set sail for heaven, or hail
    a cab to annihilation?

I

O my Captain, O my Captain
    the rocks are on the lee,
The jaws of Hell, the wicked bell
    put the fear of god up me.

What shall we do, O Captain,
    save turn to thee and cry:
'O do not leave me, but save me,
    or have a serious try.'

Ah, Annihilation Islands
    where we don't have to pray,
And no boys sing, and no bells ring,
    and never a Judgement Day.

II

It is very hard when the broken shard
    is dashed against the wall
And the fiends of Hades like flirty ladies
    pick you up, warts and all.

When it seemed lawful to be quite awful
    (how often I have been it)
Or I kissed and ran or pissed in a can
    O lord: I did not mean it.

Behold me here, so far yet near
    thy mercy and compassion,
I truly believe you ought to give
    the worthy man his ration.

No less resourceful or more remorseful
    soul than I has tried
To fly thy wrath now P. C. Death
    follows me stride for stride.

Epilogue

O I have come to the Nowhere Isles
Where the nowhere giddygoats play
    in our nowhere bars
    and our no whiskey jars
We're happy all night and all day.

For us giddygoats with our no pound notes
And no one to love at all
    we dance and we sing
    in a nowhere ring
Like an empty Nowhere Town Hall.

There's lots and lots of us never here
Like thousands and thousands of zeros
    for a lot of no people
    will certainly keep all
Nobodies happy as heroes.

O heavenly nowhere; a vacant lot
Where nobody worries one bit
    and no nosy sod
    and no guy or god
Will ever, no never find it.

Street Ballad

From high above the birds look down and sing because
   they see
the monstrous comedies they miss, living several storeys
   higher:
the dirty degradations and the gross humiliations,
they, like the gods, without pity, look down upon from a
   telephone wire.

But as they sit there high above and gaze down upon our
   brutal
short and messy circumstances, they do not see the one
who stands behind a cardboard tree examining them
   coldly
with one eye closed and the other staring along the barrel
   of a gun.

The Images of Hieronymus Bosch

In the paintings of this man
we are privileged to look upward
into a world of conditioned moral explosion.
Here all families consist of the polymorphous
inhabitants of a muddy stream
into which an electrically charged thunderbolt
has just fallen. This thunderbolt is our
consciousness of the faculty of evil
and of destruction. A religious vision
cannot produce upon the mind that observes it
a perfectly exact image of that world
because this vision imposes its own illumination
upon what it contemplates. And this illumination
exercises the extraordinary property
of evaluating or judging. Thus the objects
and subjects of the world as it is,
openly displayed to the numinous judgement
of the religious vision, receive from it
an evaluation, a series of judgements which
place each object in a sort of haloed
incandescent isolation. Subjected to
the truly religious vision all things seem
to exist in the comprehensive loneliness
of the love that, at one and the same time,
both separates them, and unites. This seemingly
universal isolation of every object
in the light of the religious eye is at heart
the prizing of it by the selective affinity:

this is that affinity's election to
love whatsoever it contemplates, and
to isolate whatsoever it loves in the one
marvellous tabernacle of the particular thing.

II

When then to the world as we know it
    slowly returns
destroyed, restored and destroyed
by its wanderings, its inexplicable voyages
    among other regions,
that mirage of what we think we see,
    then the rush of unrecognizable
wings brings with it dreams, brings us
extraordinary intimations. And we
    sit by those waters of Babylon
eternally returning, and we recognize
    the bread on the waters,
    the commonplace
like a holy vase or vessel
    coming home.

Rain at All Souls

I

The wretched Olympian, on the verge of tears
(Tears like those Housman kept locked in a drawer?)
As the geared wheel of fame and irony nears
The point of absolute loneliness, and his power
Expires like a puncture at his feet
(From simple contemplation of love lost
Without ever really being found), this incomplete
Exile sits in Oxford with a ghost.

This ghost, too living and familiar,
Sensing the homage of the lachrymae hid
Turns and beckons backwards to the bar:
Look, look, it whispers, look at what I did.
And the Olympian, from very far,
Follows it because already dead.

II

Why was this eloquent monster permitted voyage
to such illustrious stars and why was no
adequate punishment exacted from the
blonde Man-Woman? Where did he find the courage
to enter and explore mirrors so
glacial that they instructed him
how to see everything clearly, including us.
America taught him something we do not know:

Humanity includes soda jerks. He was thus
elevated into humility

by a sad love in a mad land.
And in the end all the words testify
they rose from their own opposites and
poisons became great poems in his hand.

III

The dark island that has lost its smile,
Its gravitas, and that former rigour
Of the intelligence that gave its soul
A sense of ethical direction like a figure
Drawing a clipper forward on its wings,
From this dark island he fled to find
If and what secrets of the heart of things
Hid in America. He left much behind.

And what he met was not a revelation
But the humiliation that confers
Vision upon the victim, and adulation
Of the specious kind that bleeds and blurs
All moral categories. And did he sit at last
In Oxford rain to mitigate the past?

IV

O Triumph of Love, as his flirty boy
Read out an Auden heart at Brooklyn College
And the kids gathered around just to enjoy
Sniggering at a love beyond their knowledge
And at the old avatars that spoke when he spoke
Even in loving silly letters to
The soda jerk no flattery could provoke
To pay the reciprocity that was due.

Rain at All Souls. Exile in a cloud.
What consolations can his verse provide
For tears sad Housman was not allowed?
The jaunty beachboys will turn aside
To give the love which they are not endowed
To anyone who's standing by their side.

V

The bullying scoutmaster, the great scold,
Also the petty tyrant, mathematician
Ambitious of a bishopric; also called
By some an itinerant musician;
Known to close friends as scrupulous and rather
Fond of a gin; much inclined to think
That he might have made a decent father,
Iceland was in his blood like a spiked drink.

A weakness for dirty stories about shit,
A curious notion that the Anglican
Communion has some sense in it,
He was in fact a quite uncommon man
To whom the tragic gods had seen fit
To give the gift of great metaphysician.

VI

And all the way from Brooklyn to Austria
He carried the hundredweight of his great verse
With heavier in his heart the mania
Of a love nightly getting worse and worse
As time and pain eroded everything.
How could the re-arranging alphabet
Get up in a choir and truly sing?
And yet it did. He did not forget.

There, there they are, the poems like an organ
Capable of consoling all of us
As they could not him: an organ that
We shall not hear the like of again
Until an unusually lovely chorus
Joins in a music we marvel at.

To the Memory of My Brother

I

Resuscitating before my eyes
the shade of a one-eyed one
whom I shall never see again
save as that fraternal shade:
thus memory invokes one whom
I thought never to see again
and he is here neither in flesh
or blood reminding me he is not gone
but silently sequestered among
images of what has been
like a ghost lost in an old house.
How can I speak of what is gone
when in truth he is not gone
but hangs around to supplicate
no more than the wave of a hand;
the hand that blinded that one eye.
For my writing hand can wrong
and maim not only in this verse
but in that act never to be undone
which remains and shall for ever remain
like the one line left of Agathon:
Not even the gods can undo the past.
But now I see
in this crystal and nightmare vision
that all deeds are for ever since
even forgiveness or absolution
or the old poppy cannot unmake
the Hamlet father or Absalom son.

And I must live out my time with
the crime of an eye in my right hand
like Dostoevsky foretelling that
the punishment for the crime is this:
everything cannot be undone.
And when the wind over the waste
and shrieking sea has wandered like
the criminal X searching for that
exoneration not there, that
exculpation annulled by
the deed itself, then it will see
that every thing everywhere is for ever
existing in its culpable.
We know what we do, and this
is why we cannot be forgiven.
How can we forgive the I for
inventing its own agony
above all else: to be. The womb
of waters is filled with the tears
of its own fate for ever after,
no more to be wiped away
than from my memory him.
I forgive you but not me.
You forgive me but not you.
Thus nothing is ever ever to be undone.
And in his grave my brother turns
he turns and weeps. He turns and weeps.

And now, most loved dead,
we shall not traipse again
the tenements of Ixworth Place
where we trespassed then.

And tattered at the arse
ransacked the dustbins
for ragshop junk – jamjars
and rags and rabbit skins.

All evil in that air
– the real gas of the first war –
and not a bloody soul knew
what it was all for.

We seemed to stroll the street
as though one day a great
gale would blast us back
into peace like a cancelled fête.

That was our childhood. Now
let it all be forgotten.
The view was no good and the next day's
prospect was just as rotten.

Once round the roundabout –
that's quite enough for me.
Dear man, you're the better out.
It's the devil and the Dead sea.

Shall I hail and farewell you?
I will not. I leave that to
those who will surely tell you
better than I can do.

I seek to send from no where
and to the no one you are
a love with no where to go to,
a love like the common air.

III

After so long
after so long his voice
speaks
speaks out of
a cloud
a cloud that brings
brings this
this echo of
one who is gone.

To John Heath-Stubbs

My dear blind John, the happy birds
you cannot see but hear at their
far from nefarious labours in
the once charitable skies,
those doxological and by you
so morally beloved ones
from whom, I think, upon a time
you took a canzonet or two
as they from you the bits of bread
(this faith works in a little crumb)
or entertained you in Hyde Park
with excerpts from their opera
which only winds can orchestrate,
these Puccini birds seem now
to modify for us those airs
with a conditional mistrust;
they convert my mind to a
consciousness of our culpable
and palpable liability.
But for you, I think, they sing
with unimpeded faith, because
you have walked with shadows whom
the rest of us thought murderers.
All stood in darkness, but it was
the dark that favours lovers, and
your shadows were birds and lovers whom
we cannot see or hear or touch:
they and you stand in the dark
like statues of the Gorgon's heart

and for them and you the blind
nightingales in the gale of night
perform their harmonies.
These things, which to me overcome
the reasonable mind with a
conviction of our degraded day,
must in your draped cage and cell
seem like Platonic shadows that
a ray of sunlight could dispel,
or like illusions of a mind
inebriated by the debauched
pineal eye. For you have
walked with your immolation in
a valley where the shadow was
all that a living eye could find —
no house, no double line of trees,
no sign, no moon, no road, no star,
only the lover in the shadows
standing like a statue of
the blind and mutilated heart.

To the Contessa Antonini

Still there in that pink Victorian villa she sits idly
   conversing
with the poems of Rilke and the genius of Wolfgang
   Goethe
and the flowering bushes down in her overgrown garden.
   The milkman
leaves memories of other mornings at her door, when
in a white shift out of a tousled bed she drifts down
to that exit into a wholly superfluous reality.
Her piano performs without a pianist, just as
her flowers succeed one another without a gardener, and
her days turn and return assisted only by a memory that
works like a ghost in a wheel.

To Whom Else

Had I more carefully cultivated the Horatian pentameter,
  then
this verse would live longer in your remembrance than
things being what they are, I suppose, it briefly will.
Or do I think these verses may survive you, and, well,
do I really care? I do not give a damn.
For I know that if you read them you will condemn
them simply because they were made by that over
devoted zealot who was once, not briefly, your lover.

Five Poems on the Economics of the Eumenides

'So Poverty, *thinking to alleviate*
her wretched condition by
bearing a child to Contrivance,
lay with him and conceived Love.'

Plato, *The Symposium,*
translated by Walter Hamilton

I

That the Eumenides, though superhuman, are not
supernatural

Flagellants of those guardians who attend me,
in spite of your bile and bitterness and your wholly
inhuman passion for needling those who feed you,
when will you see that Venus is always the pay day
of every uncharitable week? Acknowledging the
   exemplary
emptiness of your soul, the absolute zero of
your response to the numerology of our need,
why do you seek to prove that therefore Glastonbury
Abbey was never rebuilt? When the solicitors come
with their sweet-smelling secretaries and documents
   attesting
that they seek only to serve our purposes, why,
my dear female christs do you instantly take up an
eighteen-foot sjambok? Who are you then? Moneta?
Look down on us from the altitudes of your
Empedoclean Aetna. Only old slippers remain.

II

*That the perfect time of the Eumenides consists of the
    imperfect time*

And are those illuminations wasted that once April
so lavished upon me simply because I am absent?
Why does the lilac expend its purple exuberance
more liberally and for us alone, when we happen to be
engaged in affairs others find frivolous? Will
the morning ever again lift the curtain from my bedroom
window with quite as sunshine a finger as
when I slept with a serpent? Who has heard the humble
hedge sparrow flittering fragments of Theocritus
of an August evening when persuaded to do so only
by the solicitations of those ornithologists
who are never us? We do not hear dangerous tomorrow
we hear only farewell on its winged horse gallivanting
over the mount of Venus. We hear the fluttering
by of the butterfly but never the
tremendous error of Icarus shedding around us
feathers foretelling fall in August's farewell.
It is always somewhere and someone else.
My dear love, when clouds assemble at sunset
who, later on, gazing at them from an amorous
arbour, foresees his own suicide later in the evening?
Let us deplore the susceptibility of our simple
and single love, that love we suffer for all we
believe have survived the erosions of Eros and pure
poisonous nectar offered to us by the gods.

*That the Eumenides should be considered as
   computerized artists*

When will they proclaim an expensive orgy? When they
   foregather
around the cauldron of circumstance I discover
their purpose is cold and cruel. What they pursue is
not, as the lamb might think, a delicious meal but
the terrible spectacle of a stone not only bleeding but
demoted to a cut price, or the human image reduced
to a palette of old oil paints. When they smile I
hear their lips cracking. Children in the streets
hide behind dustbins and those of more mature years
delude themselves that these figures are forces of nature.
But are they? Are these mad ones who will not surrender
their inherent right to humiliate us really the laws
by which we die? Suppose we have invented them
out of our own necessity to find something –
anything – at least explicable in our indignity?

IV

That the Eumenides may be considered as the Muses

I have waited for you so much longer at the corner of
   nowhere
than you have any right to expect, that I cannot
   acknowledge
your presence, now, in this line. What the hell were
   you doing
in the backstreets of Kensington when I sat waiting for
   you

somewhere near Rime Intrinsica? Who waylaid you
you irridescent bitches, only too easily led by
a manicured hand into the fucking ditch?
At the corner I waited so long that now, on this evening
of rain and remorse and a single glass of foreknowledge,
I am not quite sure who you are. Are you, were you, only
the lady who holds in her hand the unicorn horn of
no cornucopia? Too often I have
stood around outside Woolworths with my gloves on
waiting for whom to appear save, Belladonna, you.

v

Poverty considered as Victory

They will not arrive by yacht or by car or by helicopter
but by the ambulance of wounds. Somewhere near
   Helicon
they encountered a bitter homecoming and I am speak-
   ing
of carpets so red that we know they were dyed with
   disasters.
Let me return to you, dirty backstreets of my childhood,
   where
poverty walked with her rags like an empress enrobing
the dignity of her bones. And as always, and again,
this serious lady attends those for whom she
reveals her intention to suffer. It is not we who
trail our perambulators and our pawn-ticketed bicycles
and our hocked blankets and bearded-female self-pity

through the streets of Economy but this white Lady
with her fake wedding ring and her striking husband
and her cold, ferocious, homicidal hatred of those
smiling Eumenides.